Ladybugs

Debbie and Brendan Gallagher

Marshall Cavendish
Benchmark
New York

This edition first published in 2012 in the United States of America by Marshall Cavendish Benchmark
An imprint of Marshall Cavendish Corporation

Website: www.marshallcavendish.us

This publication represents the opinions and views of the authors based on Debbie and Brendan Gallagher's personal experiences, knowledge, and research. The information in this book serves as a general guide only. The authors and publisher have used their best efforts in preparing this book and disclaim liability rising directly and indirectly from the use and application of this book.

Other Marshall Cavendish Offices:
Marshall Cavendish Ltd. 5th Floor, 32-38 Saffron Hill, London EC1N 8 FH, UK • Marshall Cavendish International (Asia) Private Limited, 1 New Industrial Road, Singapore 536196 • Marshall Cavendish International (Thailand) Co Ltd. 253 Asoke, 12th Flr, Sukhumvit 21 Road, Klongtoey Nua, Wattana, Bangkok 10110, Thailand • Marshall Cavendish (Malaysia) Sdn Bhd, Times Subang, Lot 46, Subang Hi-Tech Industrial Park, Batu Tiga, 40000 Shah Alam, Selangor Darul Ehsan, Malaysia

Marshall Cavendish is a trademark of Times Publishing Limited

All websites were available and accurate when this book was sent to press.

Library of Congress Cataloging-in-Publication Data

Gallagher, Debbie, 1969–
  Ladybugs / Debbie Gallagher.
    p. cm. — (Mighty minibeasts)
  Includes index.
  Summary: "Discusses the features, habitat, food, life cycle, living habits, and unique behaviors of ladybugs"--Provided by publisher.
  ISBN 978-1-60870-546-7
  1. Ladybugs—Juvenile literature. I. Title.
  QL596.C65G35 2012
  595.76'9—dc22
                                    2010040250

First published in 2011 by
MACMILLAN EDUCATION AUSTRALIA PTY LTD
15–19 Claremont Street, South Yarra 3141

Visit our website at www.macmillan.com.au or go directly to www.macmillanlibrary.com.au

Associated companies and representatives throughout the world.

Copyright Text © Debbie Gallagher 2011

Publisher: Carmel Heron
Commissioning Editor: Niki Horin
Managing Editor: Vanessa Lanaway
Editor: Tim Clarke
Proofreader: Gill Owens
Designer: Kerri Wilson (cover and text)
Page layout: Domenic Lauricella
Photo research: Legendimages
Illustrator: Gaston Vanzet
Production Controller: Vanessa Johnson

Printed in China

Acknowledgments
The authors and the publisher are grateful to the following for permission to reproduce copyright material:

Front cover photograph: A ladybird on grass © Shutterstock/ Eric Gevaert

Photographs courtesy of: Bugwood.org, photo by Gyorgy Csoka, 9, photo by Merle Shepard, Clemson University, 11 (bottom center); Corbis/Naturfoto Honal, 24; Dreamstime/ Martine De Graaf, 30, /Mashe, 20 (center right), /Nejron, 19; Entomart, 14 (bottom), 15 (both), 23, 25; iStockphoto/Chris Klotzbucher, 11 (bottom left); Minden Pictures/Foto Natura/ Jef Meul, 27; Photolibrary/Alamy/imagebroker, 18, /Alamy/ Peter Arnold, Inc., 22, /Jack Clark, 20 (top right), 21, /Ralph A Clevenger, 6, /Fabio Colombini Medeiros, 10 (bottom), /Nature Picture Library, 29, /OSF, 14 (top), /Alfred Schauhuber, 10 (top), /J S Sira, 11 (bottom right), /Andre Skonieczny, 7, /SPL/ Dr Jeremy Burgess, 17, /Ian West, 26; Shutterstock/Freerk Brouwer, 3, 16, /Eric Gevaert, 1, /Joseph Scott Photography, 11 (top right), /Alexander Maksimenko, 8 (top), /Anatoliy Samara, 13, /stoupa, 4, 11 (top left), /Studio 37, 5, /svic, 12; Forest & Kim Starr, 8 (bottom); USDA/Stephen Ausmus, 20 (top left and bottom left), /Peggy Greb, 20 (bottom right); Wikimedia Commons/Gaudete, 20 (center left).

While every care has been taken to trace and acknowledge copyright, the publisher tenders their apologies for any accidental infringement where copyright has proved untraceable. They would be pleased to come to a suitable arrangement with the rightful owner in each case.

135642

Contents

When a word is printed in **bold**, you can look up its meaning in the Glossary on page 31.

Mighty Minibeasts

Minibeasts are small animals, such as flies and spiders. Although they are small, minibeasts are a mighty collection of animals. They belong to three animal groups: arthropods, molluscs, or annelids.

	Animal Group		
	Arthropods	**Molluscs**	**Annelids**
Main Feature	Arthropods have an outer skeleton and a body that is divided into sections.	Most molluscs have a soft body that is not divided into sections.	Annelids have a soft body made up of many sections.
Examples of Minibeasts	Insects, such as ants, beetles, cockroaches, and wasps **Arachnids**, such as spiders and scorpions Centipedes and millipedes	Snails and slugs	Earthworms Leeches

More than three-quarters of all animals are minibeasts!

Ladybugs

Ladybugs are minibeasts. They belong to the arthropod group of animals. This means they have an outer skeleton and a body that is divided into sections. Ladybugs are a type of insect called a beetle.

Ladybugs are closely related to other beetles.

What Do Ladybugs Look Like?

Ladybugs have an oval body that is divided into three main parts. These parts are the head, the **thorax**, and the **abdomen**. Ladybugs have four wings and six legs.

Ladybugs have six short legs and a special shell called a pronotum (say *pro-no-tum*).

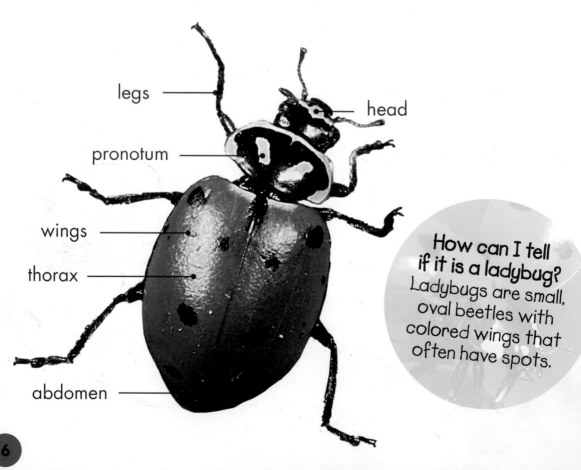

legs

head

pronotum

wings

thorax

abdomen

How can I tell if it is a ladybug? Ladybugs are small, oval beetles with colored wings that often have spots.

The top two wings on a ladybug, called elytra (say *el-ee-tra*), are hard and protect the body. The other two wings, called flight wings, are hidden underneath.

A ladybug's flight wings can only be seen when it flies.

elytra

flight wings

Different Types of Ladybugs

There are both male and female ladybugs. There are more than five thousand **species**. Ladybugs can be many colors, such as black, red, and yellow. Some have spots or patterns.

This species is called an orange ladybug and it has white spots.

These are called dark blue lady beetles. They live on the island of Hawaii.

Sometimes ladybugs from the same species can have different colors and patterns. Harlequin ladybugs have cream, orange, and black on their wings, arranged in different patterns.

These ladybugs have different colors and patterns, but they are all harlequin ladybugs.

Where in the World Are Ladybugs Found?

Ladybugs can be found all over the world, except in Antarctica, the Arctic, Greenland, and Iceland.

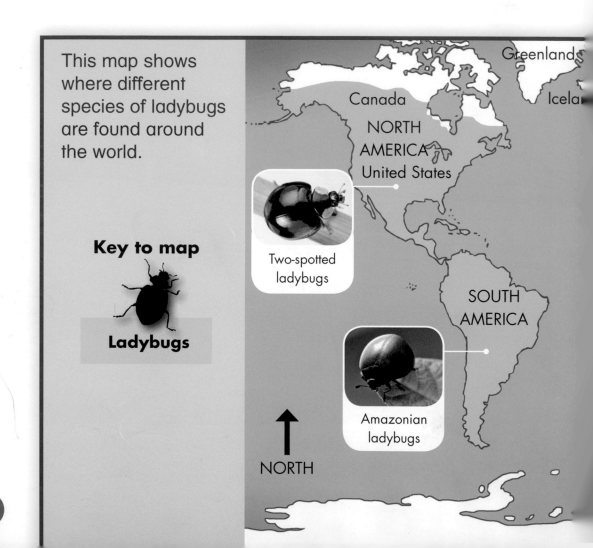

This map shows where different species of ladybugs are found around the world.

Greenland

Icela

Canada

NORTH
AMERICA
United States

Two-spotted
ladybugs

SOUTH
AMERICA

Key to map

Ladybugs

Amazonian
ladybugs

NORTH

Ladybugs do not live in places where it is too dry or too cold.

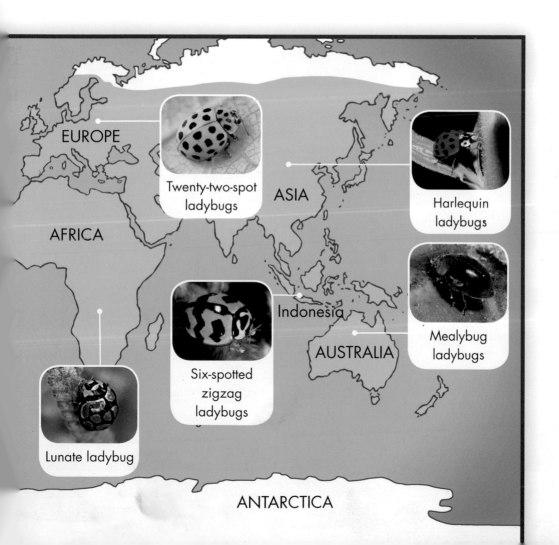

EUROPE

Twenty-two-spot ladybugs

ASIA

Harlequin ladybugs

AFRICA

Indonesia

Mealybug ladybugs

Six-spotted zigzag ladybugs

AUSTRALIA

Lunate ladybug

ANTARCTICA

Habitats of Ladybugs

Ladybugs live in all kinds of **habitats**. Some species of ladybugs prefer forests. Other species are found in grasslands, beside rivers, or in wetlands such as swamps.

This seven-spotted ladybug is living in an apple tree in a forest.

ladybug

Ladybugs live where they can find food and shelter. They are often found in gardens, in parks, and on farms.

Ladybugs can live among crops, such as in this wheat field.

ladybug

Life Cycles of Ladybugs

A life cycle diagram shows the stages of a ladybug's life, from newborn to adult.

1. A male and a female ladybug **mate**. The female lays her eggs on a plant that will be good food for the young.

4. A few days or weeks later, the pupae split and adult ladybugs come out. Their shells are soft and pale. Once their shells have dried, the ladybugs can fly away.

Ladybugs can live for up to three years.

2. After a few days or weeks, **larvae** (say *lar-vee*) hatch from the eggs. The larvae eat for several weeks. As they grow, they change their skin several times. This is called molting.

3. When the larvae are fully grown, they cling to a stem and grow a hard skin. Inside the skin, the **pupae** (say *pyoo-pee*) change into ladybugs. This is called metamorphosis (say *met-a-more-fa-siss*).

How Do Ladybugs Live?

Ladybugs are active during the day. They spend most of their lives looking for food and eating. Female ladybugs also search for a safe place to lay their eggs.

During the day ladybugs fly from plant to plant in search of food.

Ladybugs live near each other, but not in family or community groups. They need to live near each other so they can mate.

Several ladybugs will often live together on the same plant.

Ladybug Homes

Ladybugs do not live in homes such as nests. At night they rest in different places, such as under tree bark or on plant stems.

These ladybugs are resting inside a tree stump.

ladybugs

When ladybugs need to shelter from the rain, they can rest on the underside of a leaf. Ladybugs can also hide in small spaces on buildings.

By sheltering under leaves, ladybugs can stay dry when it rains.

Ladybug Food

Many types of ladybugs eat insects, such as aphids. A few types of ladybugs only eat plants and mildew, which is a plant disease.

Foods That Ladybugs Eat

Aphids		Scale insects	
Flower **pollen** and **nectar**		Honeydew and fruit juice	
Mildew		Beetle eggs	

Ladybugs eat all the food they find on a plant. Once ladybugs have eaten all the food on a plant, they look for a new plant.

Some ladybugs can eat up to forty aphids in a day.

Why Do Ladybugs Hibernate?

Some ladybugs hibernate during the winter. This means that they spend a long time resting when it is cold. They hibernate because there is not much food in the wintertime.

Some ladybugs hibernate in large groups.

When the weather becomes warm again, ladybugs wake up and start to search for food. Ladybugs eat lots of food in summer to keep them alive while they hibernate.

Groups of hibernating ladybugs move around again once the weather warms up.

Threats to the Survival of Ladybugs

Ladybugs are threatened by other animals. Many **predators** feed on ladybugs and their larvae, pupae, and eggs. These predators include:

- birds, such as sparrows
- spiders
- insects, such as ants and other beetles
- other ladybugs.

Ants are predators that feed on ladybugs.

Ladybugs protect themselves from predators by:
- pretending to be dead
- using their bright colors to warn predators that they taste bad
- squirting out a bad-tasting liquid when they are threatened.

This ladybug is pretending to be dead so the spider will not want to eat it.

Pest Ladybugs

Some types of ladybug can be pests, causing problems for other species. Harlequin ladybugs are spreading into Europe from their home in Asia. They are taking over the habitats of **native** ladybugs.

Harlequin ladybugs cause problems for humans by coming inside houses in large groups to hibernate.

Harlequin ladybugs eat the food that the native ladybugs eat. When this food runs out, harlequin ladybugs eat other ladybugs and their eggs.

Harlequin ladybugs eat other ladybugs, such as the twenty-two-spot ladybug.

twenty-two-spot ladybug

harlequin ladybug

Ladybugs and the Environment

Ladybugs are an important part of the **environment** they live in. Ladybugs feed on other animals and on plants, and many animals feed on them. This is shown in a food web.

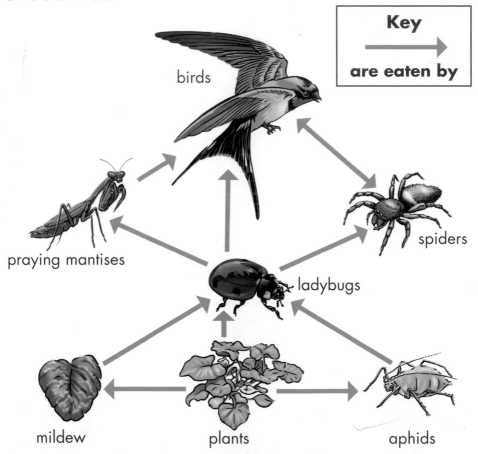

Key

→

are eaten by

birds

praying mantises

spiders

ladybugs

mildew

plants

aphids

This food web shows what ladybugs eat and what eats them.

Ladybugs eat insects that are pests on farms and in gardens, such as aphids. People put ladybugs on crops in their gardens so they eat these pests.

Ladybugs help the environment by eating aphids, which damage plants.

Tips for Watching Ladybugs

These tips will help you to watch ladybugs:

- Look for ladybugs in your own garden or at a local park.
- Check under leaves, in hedges, or on tree trunks.
- Use a magnifying glass to look at the tiny larvae or eggs.
- During winter, groups of ladybugs sometimes hide under loose tree bark or window sills.

Look but do not touch! Watch ladybugs without touching them to see where they go and what they do.

Ladybugs can often be seen on flowers.

Glossary

abdomen — The end section of an insect's body.

arachnids — Eight-legged animals, such as spiders, that are part of the arthropod group.

environment — The air, water, and land that surround us.

habitats — Areas in which animals are naturally found.

larvae — The young of an insect.

mate — Join together to produce young.

native — Belonging to a particular habitat or country.

nectar — A sweet liquid made by flowers.

pollen — Yellow powder found on flowers.

predators — Animals that hunt other animals for food.

pupae — What insect larvae turn into before becoming adults.

species — Groups of animals or plants that have similar features.

thorax — The part of the body between the head and abdomen.

Index